GAME CHANGERS

GAME CHANGERS

Mio Debnam

Collins

Contents

Key inventions in history

safety bike

Kinetograph and
Kinetoscope camera

1885

1891

1888

Kodak camera

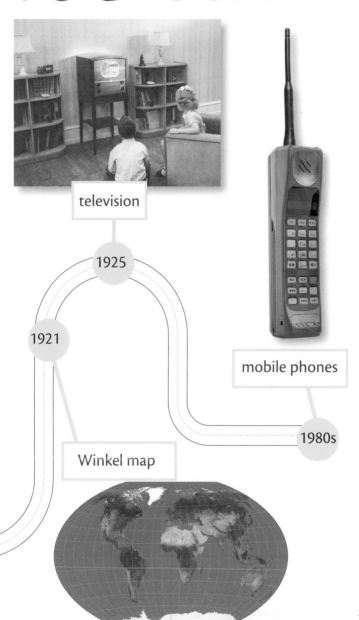

television

1925

1921

Winkel map

mobile phones

1980s

3

Chapter 1
Then, now and the future

Introduction

Look around you, at the things at home or school. Think about the things that you use every day – from getting up, to going to bed.

Now imagine you have a time machine which can transport you backwards and forwards in time.

How different do you think your life would be if you went back 300 years to 1725? How about back 100 years to 1925? What if we went forward 100 years to 2125?

London in 1725

If you went back in time to London in 1725, something you'd notice right away would be the smell!

Flushing toilets didn't exist. Most people in the city shared an indoor "privy" which was a board you sat on, with a hole over a bucket.

The buckets were supposed to be emptied into a **cesspit** ... but sometimes people just threw the contents out of their windows, so the unpaved streets were dirty and stank!

a privy

There was no running water either, so
most people didn't wash very often, adding to
the general smell.

The streets were dark at night. Most homes were
dark too, lit only by log fires and candles.

Evenings would have been quite different in
those days. Many people went to bed early, when
it got dark, and got up when it was light outside.
There was no television, no internet … and not many
books, either, as many people couldn't read or write!

If you had a message, you had to tell that person directly – or write a letter. Letters had to be delivered by hand or on horseback, as cars hadn't been invented yet.

Rich people had plenty of time for entertainment. They played games and did sports.

Some leisure activities were enjoyed by everyone – such as walks in "pleasure gardens" or parks, and visits to fairs. The theatre was also open to everyone – though poor people had to stand to watch the plays!

a pleasure garden

7

Life in 1925

If you'd travelled back to 1925, you might have found yourself staying with a well-off family, in one of the very first homes in London to have been fitted with electricity. The gaslights in this home would have been replaced by electric lights which were much brighter.

The streets were well lit too – with a system of gas lamps. In addition, in some areas of London, there were some huge super-bright electric lights high up in the sky.

In this home, the kitchen would have had a gas stove similar to those found in modern kitchens. An icebox kept things cool using blocks of ice. The bathroom also had running water, and flush toilets which were connected to the **sewer**.

In the evenings, many families listened to the radio for entertainment. They may have heard about the invention of the television in October 1925 on the radio, though most people wouldn't have one for **decades**!

The increasing use of electricity also changed entertainment. Going to the theatre to watch a play was still popular, but by 1925, there were also hundreds of cinemas or "electric theatres" in London. Cinemas were cheap enough that most people could afford to go, including children.

Most cinemas were fairly basic and just screened films, but some of the fancier ones also had live shows, with music, acting or dancing, before the film!

There were buses and trains, and trams – so people were able to travel more, and further than they'd previously been able to. Roads were paved, making travel with car, bike or foot much easier than in 1725. There were good maps available too, so you wouldn't get lost.

The well-off even went overseas on ships and planes.

And ordinary people were able to record their trips and special moments for the first time with their Kodak cameras!

Life in 2125

No one knows what our homes and lives will be like in the future, but we can make some guesses based on inventions which are already in use.

It's likely that everything in your home will be connected to the internet, and linked. You'll be able to control everything, even if you aren't there!

When you arrive home, on your hoverboard, you may be able to unlock your door and turn the lights on just by thinking about it.

All houses will probably be **energy-efficient**. The walls might be covered with a special **flexible** material that glows to provide lighting, or lights up like a TV or computer screen!

In the future, we may not even need to phone or travel to contact someone. Instead we might be able to meet up as holograms – moving, talking 3D **projections** that look almost like real people!

Will any of these ideas come true? It'll be interesting to find out!

Necessity = inventions

Have you heard of the saying, "necessity is the mother of invention"? It means that when humans need something to make their lives better or easier, they will invent something to fill that need!

As you have read, there have been many scientific discoveries and inventions that have completely changed the way people live. And this wave of invention is still happening. All inventions start off as ideas. Sometimes, when an inventor first has an idea, the right **technology** isn't in place to make it happen. Sometimes, years, or even decades, pass before the idea becomes a reality.

Many things that make our lives easier today are also the result of an early invention which has been improved over the years by other inventors. This book will show you how some things have changed from a simple idea, to what we have today!

Small inventions that made a BIG difference

Zip

This small but mighty invention from 1913 saves us valuable time!

Can opener

The can opener was invented nearly 50 years after cans were first invented! The first cans were made of much thicker metal and were opened using a hammer and chisel!

Sliced bread

Did you know that
bread wasn't always
sold sliced
like this?
It wasn't until
1928, when an American
man created a bread slicing machine that
you could buy bread already sliced!

Plasters

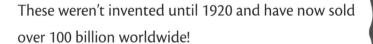

These weren't invented until 1920 and have now sold
over 100 billion worldwide!

Chapter 2
On the move!

What do cars, buses and bicycles have in common?

They all get us from one place to another quickly and wouldn't exist if the wheel hadn't been invented around 6,000 years ago!

Did you know?

Before the wheel, people laid logs on the ground, and put heavy loads on them. These "rollers" helped them push the loads along.

At first, wheels were solid wooden disks, often made by slicing tree trunks!

They were used in wheelbarrows, as well as carts and wagons, pulled by strong animals such as oxen.

Unfortunately, solid wheels were very heavy, so a lighter wheel was invented, which had rims, spokes and a hub with a hole for the axle.

Because these wheels were lighter, smaller animals such as horses could be used to pull these new vehicles.

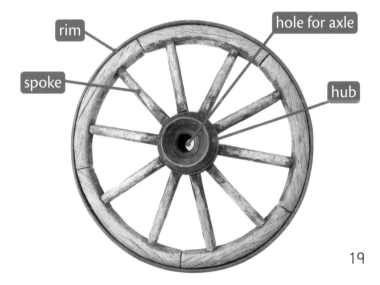

rim

hole for axle

spoke

hub

Although the invention of the wheel made it easier for people to transport things, and travel around, vehicles with wheels still needed animals to pull them!

That changed in 1817 when a German inventor invented the *laufmaschine* which means "running-machine"! His wooden machine looked similar to the bikes we know today but had no pedals. Instead, the rider sat on the seat and used their feet to push it along!

Say it!
laufmaschine:
"lowf-mash-een-a"

Riding the laufmaschine was faster than walking or running. But, because it was heavy, hard to steer and didn't have any brakes, it was difficult and dangerous to use. It never became very popular.

the laufmaschine

Over the next few decades, many different human-powered machines were invented. None of them were very successful.

Then about 50 years after the laufmaschine was introduced, an iron, two-wheeled machine was invented in France. It had pedals that turned the front wheel.

Very quickly these "bicycles", as they were called, became popular in Europe.

The wheels of these early bikes had wooden spokes and a metal rim, and didn't have rubber tyres like modern bikes do. This meant riders felt every bump in the road! This earned these uncomfortable bikes the nickname "bone-shakers"!

Bicycle design continued to change – the front wheel became far larger than the back wheel. These bikes, called the "penny-farthing", were faster and less bumpy than the bone-shaker.

the bone-shaker

However, penny-farthings were hard to get on and off, as the seat was so high. Riders found them hard to control and often flew over the handlebars if they braked hard or hit a bump! These bikes were also expensive, so were mostly popular with well-off young men!

the penny-farthing

Did you know?

The penny-farthing bike gets its name from two British coins – the large "penny" and the much smaller "farthing", as the front wheel was much bigger than the back!

penny   farthing

23

The "safety bike", invented in the mid-1880s, was an instant success. By the 1890s, it was the most popular bike design being used.

Both of the wheels were a similar size, and air-filled tyres made the ride less bumpy. You could steer the bike with the handlebars, and stop it with the brakes. The pedals and chain turned the back wheel, making it even faster than the penny-farthing. It was also easier to ride and more stable!

The safety bike was lighter and less expensive than the penny-farthing, so thousands of people bought them. Many women started cycling too. In order to ride more easily, women started wearing knee-length, loose trousers called "bloomers" instead of the long skirts most women wore at the time.

a female cyclist in bloomers with a safety bike

Improvements continued to be introduced, including gears, which made cycling less tiring.

But as more trams, trains and cars became available, fewer people cycled. By 1920, cycling had become less popular.

Luckily, bikes continued to be produced and improved through the decades.

Bikes have recently become more popular again, as people have realised that cycling is a quick and efficient way to get around, which creates no air pollution and is good exercise!

Many cities around the world now have bicycling lanes and bike-sharing systems, where you can borrow a bike for a short period, whenever you need it.

It seems clear that bikes are here to stay!

In 2017, Amanda Coker decided to break the world record for the greatest distance travelled on a bicycle in one year. She got up at 4 o'clock every morning and rode her bike round and round a park in Florida, US, for about 13 hours every day.

She cycled through rain and shine – even riding during a big storm.

In one year, she managed to travel 139,326 kilometres – a distance of almost three and a half times around the world!

Most people enjoy just going for bike rides, but for more serious cyclists, there are many sports they can get involved in.

For example, there are long-distance road races, such as the Tour de France, which takes three weeks to finish and covers 3,600 kilometres!

There are shorter races too, called "sprint cycling". These take place in **velodromes**, on special tracks that tilt up at the sides.

Adventurous cyclists can enjoy off-road racing, or BMX biking too!

Tour de France

BMX bikes are a special type of bicycle which are used in the Olympic sports of BMX racing and BMX freestyle. They are smaller and lighter than normal bikes, which makes them easier to do stunts with.

BMX freestyle is particularly exciting to watch. Competitors have to ride around a course full of ramps, jumps and curved slopes, doing as many risky, difficult stunts as they can in one minute, to impress the judges!

Amazing bikes around the world

Some bikes might be more useful than others ... take a look at some of the most amazing bikes invented!

Here is a bike you can lie down on!
The recumbent bike was invented in Switzerland.

This is the longest bicycle in the world, from Australia!

The "Conference" bike from Holland can seat seven people!

Walter Nilsson in Los Angeles, US, with his creation, the Uno-Wheel!

Chapter 3
Lost?

People have been **navigating** around Earth, and making maps, for thousands of years.

Maps show us where and how far apart places are. Mapmakers have used maps to show where food sources are, or where danger lies, as well as showing how to get from one place to another.

Did you know?

One of the oldest maps discovered is more than 2,500 years old! The map – of ancient Babylon – was carved onto a small clay tablet.

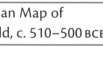

Babylonian Map of the World, c. 510–500 BCE

These days, almost all of the land on Earth has been **mapped**. That's partly because modern **satellites** can take photos from space, showing difficult-to-reach places, which mapmakers can study and use.

a satellite over Earth

In the past, however, there were many unknown places. People had no way of knowing what, if anything, was over a mountain or across an ocean, unless they went there themselves!

Early maps were created by explorers who went on **expeditions** to places they didn't know.

The ancient Egyptians were among the earliest sea explorers. They set sail around 5,000 years ago and explored the coastline near Egypt.

The biggest problem ancient explorers like them faced was getting lost at sea.

People travelling across land could look for "landmarks", or things they recognised, such as lakes, mountains, or buildings. But when they were sailing on the open seas, they could only see the sky and the waves!

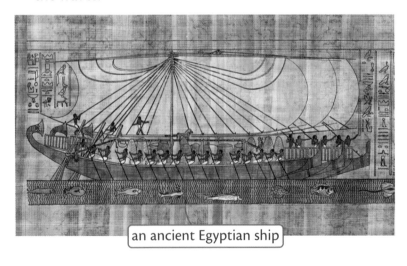

an ancient Egyptian ship

Studying the position of the stars and the sun helped ancient explorers work out which direction to go. But when it was stormy or cloudy, they could easily go off course!

The invention of the compass – an instrument that showed directions – about 1,000 years ago, changed everything.

Did you know?
A compass has a "needle" which is magnetic. This needle always turns so that one end points to the North Pole, and the other to the South Pole, so it's easy to tell which direction you're going.

Animals with a built-in compass!

Homing pigeons can find their way home even if released somewhere they've never been before.

Salmon spend years living in the ocean. However, when ready to breed, they travel thousands of kilometres to the same river where they were born.

Similarly, monarch butterflies, geese, whales, wildebeest and other animals travel vast distances when they migrate to warmer places, or areas with more food. They travel back as the seasons change.

a monarch butterfly

a grey whale

Animals can't use maps. So, how do they travel without getting lost? Earth has a magnetic field running from the North Pole to the South Pole.

Scientists believe that some animals can detect and use Earth's magnetic field to work out where to go.

It's thought that a magnetic mineral (called magnetite) in their bodies may act like a built-in compass. This helps them work out which way is north, and to navigate.

Compasses helped explorers cross oceans and find lands they didn't know existed. These explorers helped to make maps more accurate.

But a world map has to show all parts of Earth at once – as if the globe was cut from north to south, then flattened.

Imagine drawing the countries of the world on a blown-up balloon, then cutting it from top to bottom along one side. To make this opened-up balloon into a flat, rectangular map, you'd have to pull the cut edges out and stretch them to fit.

This stretching to flatten the map **distorts** the shape and size of many countries.

On the "Mercator" map (widely used in the past by sailors), countries near the equator are about the correct shape and size, but those further away are shown as larger than they are.

Africa looks the same size as Greenland, but is actually 14 times larger, and Antarctica looks long and huge, but it's round, and less than half the size of Africa!

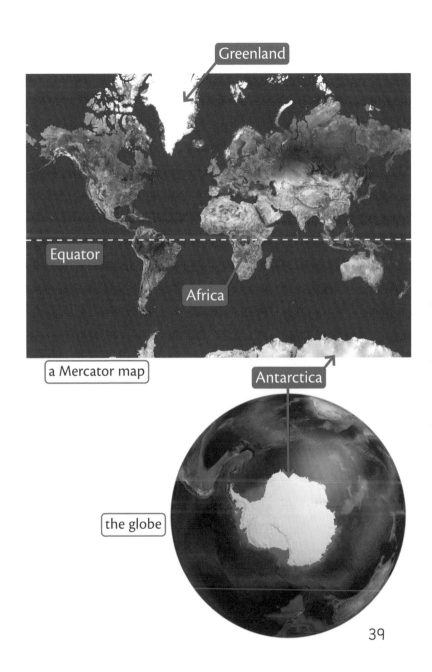

Greenland

Equator

Africa

a Mercator map

Antarctica

the globe

Newer map types, such as the "Winkel Tripel" and "AuthaGraph", have tried to correct some of these inaccuracies.

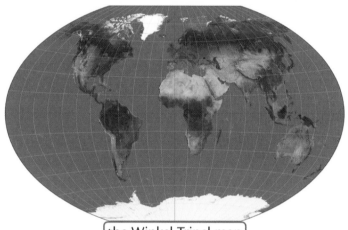

the Winkel Tripel map

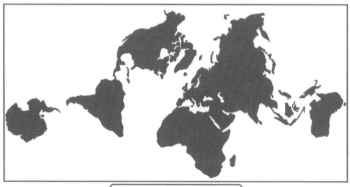

an AuthaGraph map

The AuthaGraph map was created in 1999 by Hajime Narukawa. Unlike most other maps, the equator is not shown as a horizontal line across the centre of the map.

The shape and sizes of the continents are less distorted than in earlier maps, and it shows Antarctica's correct shape, but even this map isn't perfect!

Unlike large-scale maps, maps of smaller areas can be extremely accurate, and maps of all types continue to be very useful to those who are planning trips, or already travelling.

Paper maps are bulky, a little fragile and sometimes can be expensive, but they never run out of batteries, and don't need an internet connection to work!

Despite that, these days many people use map apps on their mobile phones, rather than a paper map.

Map apps on phones do have a huge advantage, however, in that they can track you, using GPS. This allows you to see where you are as you move along, and the app can even tell you the best way to go to get to your destination.

Did you know?

GPS stands for "Global Positioning System". A GPS machine listens for signals from satellites in space, and uses the information to calculate where you are on Earth.

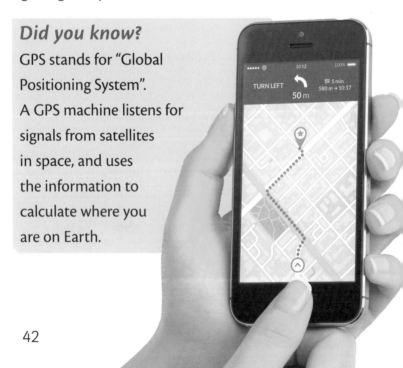

Treasure maps are only found in books and movies, but millions of adults and children around the world enjoy finding "treasure" of sorts, when they play geocaching. Players use the geocaching app to decide where to go, then use their phone GPS and clues, to find the hidden "cache" or "treasure".

Players sign the logbook that's with the cache to say they've found it, then hide it again for the next person to discover!

finding a cache

Inventions inspired by nature: spider glass

Every year millions of birds are injured or killed when they crash into windows. Glass is see-through, so birds don't realise it's there.

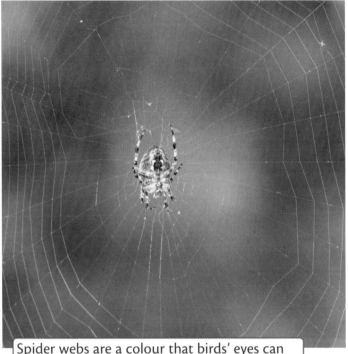

Spider webs are a colour that birds' eyes can see clearly. But it is almost invisible to humans.

To keep birds safe, a company has invented "spider glass". This is covered in a web of lines that birds can see but humans can't!

what birds see

what we see

Chapter 4
Smile!

These days, taking a photo is so easy that people all around the world take millions, every minute of every day. Did you know that in the time it took you to read this paragraph, about one million photos were taken?

In the past, people wanting a picture of themselves had to get a portrait painted!

But around 200 years ago, in the early 1820s, French inventor Joseph Niépce discovered a way to create pictures without paint.

He called these pictures "heliographs". They're considered to be the first-ever photograph. Modern cameras take a photo in the click of a button. Niépce's first heliograph, however, is thought to have taken eight hours, or more, to create!

The thing being photographed and the camera had to remain absolutely still until the picture was ready – which took hours. Because of this, heliographs were mostly of scenery rather than people!

the first heliograph: view from Niépce's window

Did you know?

The words "heliograph" and "photograph" are made up of ancient Greek words, for sun (*helios*), light (*photo*) and drawing (*graph*).

Say it!

Niépce: "nee-eps"
heliograph: "hee-lee-oa-graph"

Early heliographs were fuzzy and not very detailed. Niépce worked on his method, and his picture quality improved. But it still sometimes took days to take a picture!

By the time Niépce died in 1833, he had a partner called Louis Daguerre. Daguerre knew that the biggest problem with Niépce's method was that it took too long to capture the image.

This was because it took a long time for the chemicals on the heliographic plate to react to the small amount of light entering the camera.

Did you know?

Unlike photographs, which are printed on paper, heliographs were made on metal painted with light-sensitive chemicals (the heliographic plate).

Early cameras were just a box, with a small hole and a glass lens at the front! The box was sealed, so light could only enter through the lens.

To take a picture, a "heliographic plate" was slotted inside the camera. The light from the scene would enter through the lens and **react** with the chemicals on the plate to form a picture.

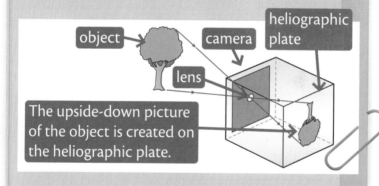

object
camera
heliographic plate
lens

The upside-down picture of the object is created on the heliographic plate.

Daguerre experimented with several different chemicals to find a mixture which would react more quickly. By 1839, Daguerre had achieved this.

Camera lenses were improving too, and soon it became possible to take a picture in under a minute. That was much quicker, but the people in the photo still had to use a head brace to keep themselves still so the photo wouldn't be blurry!

These pictures, which he called "daguerrotypes" were sharper and far more detailed than heliographs.

In 1839, English scientist William Henry Fox Talbot announced that he'd discovered a way to make pictures.

Talbot used similar light-**reactive** chemicals to Daguerre, but he painted them on paper, not metal.

Talbot's "negative"

Daguerrotypes were created on highly-polished metal plates. One side of the plate was coated with light-reactive chemicals, before it was put quickly into a camera.

When the picture had formed, the plate was washed in a special bath. This "fixed" the picture, so it wouldn't be affected any further by light. Daguerrotypes were often kept in glass-fronted frames to protect them and stop them from fading.

Every daguerrotype was unique – unlike modern photographs, you couldn't make copies.

a daguerrotype

Say it!

daguerre: "da-gair"

daguerrotype: "da-gair-o-type"

Daguerre's method resulted in a finished picture, but Talbot's created a **translucent** "negative". This meant the picture was dark where you'd expect it to be light, and vice versa. Talbot used these negatives to print pictures on paper. He called the pictures "calotypes".

Daguerrotypes continued to become more popular around the world. Unfortunately, you had to make one daguerreotype at a time. You couldn't make copies of a picture like you can now! Copies could be made using Talbot's method, but the pictures were fuzzy. Luckily, other inventors worked on and improved Talbot's method. Soon it became possible to take one picture and then make several copies, which were as sharp as daguerrotypes! Daguerrotyping quickly fell out of fashion.

a calotype

In 1888, an American, George Eastman, revolutionised photography by inventing the Kodak camera.

Until then, most people didn't have their own camera, because the camera and other equipment were expensive, large and difficult to use. They used a trained photographer instead.

Kodak cameras were small, affordable, and contained a flexible roll of film. You could take 100 photos, before sending the camera to the company. Kodak printed your photos, then sent them and your camera with new film back to you.

THE
KODAK

Is a Hand Camera especially designed for Amateurs. It is the most compact instrument made, and with it the largest number of exposures can be made with the least number of operations.
PICTURES SQUARE OR ROUND.
NO PREVIOUS KNOWLEDGE OF PHOTOGRAPHY IS NECESSARY.
"YOU PRESS THE BUTTON,
WE DO THE REST."

ILLUSTRATED CATALOGUE FREE.

The Eastman Photo Materials Co., Ltd.,
115, Oxford Street, London, W.
Paris : 4, Place Vendôme.   Nice : Place Grimaldi.

Kodak cameras made it easy for anyone to take photos. This made photography popular.

Soon newer cameras were invented: from pocket-sized "point-and-click" automatics that control the settings themselves, to Polaroids, to complicated cameras for trained photographers.

Film quality improved too. When colour film was introduced in 1936, it quickly became more popular than black-and-white film.

However, the basics of photography didn't change for over 100 years. A camera was used to create negative images on film. The film was developed and photos were printed on paper.

Another huge change happened in 1975 – digital photography was invented.

Now, light entering the camera wasn't recorded as a picture on film, but as electrical signals.

Digital cameras became common in the mid-1990s. People loved being able to look at and share their photos, without needing to print them!

The introduction of mobile phones with built-in cameras, in 2000, changed things again. Nowadays, nearly all photos are taken with a mobile phone!

Did you know?
What do people take photos of most?
Food, dogs and selfies!

Beauty inventions through history

Throughout the years, the beauty industry has created and sold some interesting-looking machines! Would you want to try either of these?

Dimple maker

This dimple maker is from the 1930s.

Hair permer

The hair permer was designed to make someone's hair wavy or curly! This is a hair permer from 1905. Luckily, it's much easier to get your hair permed nowadays!

Chapter 5
Action!

These days you can see moving pictures in adverts, videos, movies, television and many other places. They're so common that it seems incredible that they were only invented about 100 years ago! We have moving pictures thanks to Eadweard Muybridge. In 1878, he arranged 12 cameras in a row, and set them to take photos in turn, as a horse galloped by. He did this to check if a horse took all of its hooves off the ground while galloping! (It does!)

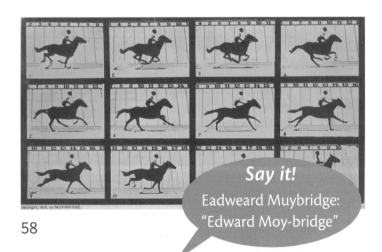

Say it!
Eadweard Muybridge:
"Edward Moy-bridge"

58

Muybridge took many series of photos of things in motion.

Later, he also invented a machine called the Zoopraxiscope – on which he could show his photos quickly one after the other. Showing them like this made them look like they were moving.

Muybridge used a separate camera to take each picture. As he only had 24 cameras in all, he could only capture a few seconds of movement!

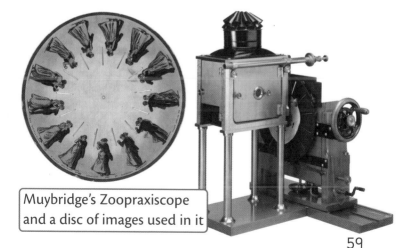

Muybridge's Zoopraxiscope and a disc of images used in it

Flipbooks have a picture on each page which is slightly different from the page before. If you flip the pages quickly, it will seem

flipbook

as though the objects in the picture are moving! That's because when we see a series of still pictures flick past, our eyes and brains "knit" them together so it seems like they're moving.

Movies work in the same way – with 24 or more still pictures (called "frames") being displayed every second on the screen.

In 1891, Thomas Edison invented the Kinetograph camera, Kinetoscope and phonograph.

The Kinetograph camera took 40 photos a second and worked in a similar way to modern movie cameras. The movies produced were only a few seconds long.

People could watch these movies on a machine called the Kinetoscope. There was a peephole on top of the machine they could look through. They wore headphones so they could hear the sound played on the phonograph (an early record player).

Kinetoscopes became so popular that crowds gathered in Kinetoscope halls to watch these short films.

using the Kinetoscope

Say it!
Kinetograph: kin-net-oh-graph
Kinetoscope: kin-net-oh-scope
phonograph: phone-oh-graph

French inventors, Auguste and Louis Lumière, were inspired by the Kinetoscope. They invented a machine called a Cinématographe. It was a movie camera which was also a **projector**, that allowed the movie to be shown on a wall to many people at once.

Say it!
Lumière: loo-mee-air
Cinématographe:
sin-ai-mat-o-graph

the Cinématographe

Did you know?
The Cinématographe was about the weight of a small dog, while the original Kinetograph weighed as much as a horse!

The Lumière's movies were jerkier than Edison's … but the Cinématographe was lighter and easier to carry around.

Edison's Kinetograph was so bulky, he could only shoot movies in his studio, but the Lumière brothers were able to travel around France, shooting and showing their movies anywhere – even outdoors!

Their invention quickly became widely used in Europe, then in the US. But these movies were still extremely short, and didn't have a story.

Seeing the Cinématographe's success, Edison's company quickly developed a Kinetograph camera to carry around, and started making very short movies of everyday life, like the Lumière brothers.

Did you know?

In the US, moving pictures were known as "movies", but in the UK they were called "films" as they were shot on film.

They also started making a projector called the Vitascope – which allowed their movies to be seen by a wider audience. By 1900, many others had become involved in making movies.

Gradually, movies became longer, and they began to tell a story, rather than being a random collection of scenes. Movie makers became skilled in filming and editing. All sorts of movies, from comedies to documentaries to dramas, were made. By 1920, it was big business!

Did you know?

Until 1927, movies were silent. They were accompanied by music played by a live band, or on a phonograph!

Changing to movies with sound – called the "talkies" – was difficult and expensive, as new equipment had to be fitted in cinemas.

But by the early 1930s, most movies had sound and they were starting to be in colour too!

At about the same time as movie technology was being developed, inventors were also working on a new type of machine to show moving pictures, called the television. This didn't use film – but instead used an electrical signal to produce a picture!

watching TV in the 1940s

The first televisions were made in the late 1930s and they could only show black-and-white pictures. But by the early 1950s, colour TVs were being produced too.

In 1960, there were only a couple of TV channels – the US had three, the UK had two.

Families made time to watch their favourite shows when they were shown, as they couldn't record them, or stream them later, as we can now.

In the UK, the number of hours that TV stations were allowed to broadcast shows was strictly controlled. Until 1957, the TV stations went off between 6 o'clock and 7 o'clock in the evening, to allow parents to put their children to bed!

Since the 1960s, things have changed completely. Several inventions have come and gone, including **video cassettes**, which allowed people to record TV programmes and rent movies to watch at home.

Videos were replaced by DVDs, which in turn were replaced by **streaming** channels. These days you don't need a cinema or even a TV to watch films.

In fact, now almost anyone can shoot and show mini-movies, with a mobile phone or tablet. Edison would be amazed!

Early contact lenses

Some people wear soft, light, plastic "contact lenses" on the surface of their eyes instead of glasses, to correct their vision.

But did you know that contact lenses were actually invented over 200 years ago?

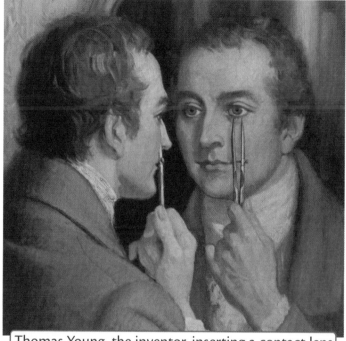

Thomas Young, the inventor, inserting a contact lens

Plastic hadn't been invented yet, so the first contact lenses were made of glass. They were so heavy, they kept falling out and had to be stuck in with hot wax ... ouch!

Chapter 6
Hello?

These days, mobile phones are so common that nearly all young adults in the UK and the US, as well as many other parts of the world, own one! Experts think that more than two-thirds of all the people on Earth have a mobile phone! Telephones are so common that it's hard to imagine being without them …

Sending a message to someone was hard until the 1840s when the telegraph was invented. People were then able to use the telegraph to send messages called telegrams, almost instantly, to people far away. Messages were converted to Morse code and sent using bursts of electricity through a system of telegraph wires.

By 1866, there was even an undersea telegraph line between the US and Europe.

Telegraph operators who sent or received telegrams had to learn Morse code.

Morse code turned every letter or number into a pattern of dots and dashes. Operators gave the telegraph button a short tap to send a dot, or held the button down to send a dash.

Using this code, words and sentences could be spelt out – and decoded at the other end.

tapping out a message in Morse code using an old telegraph machine

Telegraphs allowed messages to be sent over long distances almost instantly, for the first time.

They soon became a popular method of communication. They remained that way for over 100 years, even after the invention of the telephone, as it was less expensive than an overseas call! You can still send and receive telegrams in many countries.

1870s telegraph operators

Did you know?
Once printed, the telegrams were hand-delivered by uniformed delivery boys on bikes or motorbikes.

Almost immediately, inventors started trying to improve how the telegraph worked. One of those people was Alexander Graham Bell, who wanted to find a way to send several messages at once along the same line.

He invented a "harmonic telegraph". This involved sending several signals at once which could be received as different musical tones. Each tone represented a different message.

This gave him the idea of a machine that would become the telephone!

On 14th February 1876, Bell registered an invention that would allow speech to be heard across a telegraph wire.

The model of the telephone Bell registered didn't actually work properly, but within a month, he'd fixed it, and made the world's first phone call.

one of the earliest phones invented

Did you know?
When you register an invention, you get a "patent". This tells everyone that you are the original inventor of the object.

Twenty years before Bell, an Italian inventor called Antonio Meucci made a machine that could send his voice along a wire, so it could be heard at the other end. Sadly, he didn't patent his invention.

Another man, Elisha Gray, went to patent a similar invention to Bell's just hours after him. Gray lost the legal battle about who invented the telephone first.

Bell calling long distance in 1892

The first few phones were directly connected together by wire ... but within two years, the first telephone exchange had opened in the US.
Each phone had a line going into a switchboard at the exchange.

operators working at telephone switchboards

Callers contacted the exchange by pressing the telephone hook. The switchboard operator asked them who they wanted to speak to, then plugged in wires to connect the caller's phone with the phone of the person they were calling!

In the early days, phone calls weren't very private. Those without a phone had to make calls on public phones, for example, in shops ... and many houses shared the same phone line. These were called "party lines".

hook

This meant that your neighbours could listen in on your phone conversations if they wanted!

You also had to wait till your neighbour finished, before you could use the phone.

Did you know?
Bell introduced telephones to the UK in 1878.

Homing pigeons have been used as messengers for centuries, due to their ability to find their way home from anywhere.

They were especially useful in wartime. Armies carried pigeons with them, releasing the birds when they had secret reports to send home, which they didn't want the enemy to see!

The report was put in a tiny tube on the pigeon's leg.

These messages were printed so small that they were sometimes read with a microscope!

message

Many people, including Edison, were involved with the development of the phone. How telephones and switchboards looked and worked, quickly improved.

1900s

A major invention was the dial telephone. This allowed people to phone each other without having to speak to an operator.

1930s

Soon after, a new handset combined the part you spoke into and the part you listened to into one. Telephone shapes changed dramatically.

1950s

Next came push-button phones, followed by cordless home phones and car phones.

1980s

dial phones through the years

The first mobile phones, in the 1980s, were almost as big and heavy as a brick ... and the batteries didn't last long! Luckily, smaller phones that allowed text messaging and simple games followed.

In 2007, the Apple iPhone changed everything. Now, most mobiles are smartphones with touchscreens, that allow you to do almost anything your computer, TV, camera and road map can do, AND make calls too!

Inventions inspired by nature: hook and loop fasteners

While walking in a wood, in 1948, a Swiss inventor noticed that he and his dog were covered in burrs.

the burrs were stuck tightly and were hard to remove

Burrs are plant seed pods.

He examined the burrs under a microscope and discovered that they were covered in hooked spines.

This gave him an idea for a fastener which had hooks on one side and loops on the other. The hooks and loops could be joined securely, but were easy to pull apart.

He'd invented Velcro®!

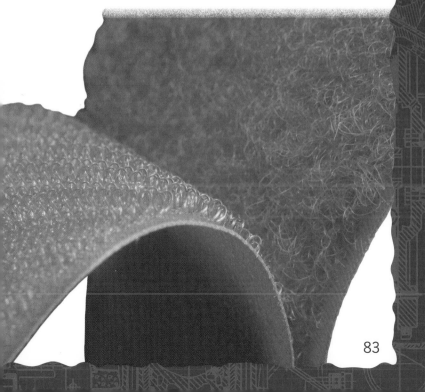

Glossary

cesspit a pit in which sewage and other waste is thrown away

decades periods of ten years

distorts pulls out of shape

energy-efficient doesn't use too much electricity

expeditions journeys with a purpose

flexible can be bent

mapped has been studied in order to make a map

navigating finding a course

projections pictures that are produced

projector the machine that makes the projection

react/reactive when something changes due to light being shone on it

satellites human-made machine flying around Earth

sewer a human-made system of tunnels for carrying used and dirty water away

streaming transmitting, watching or listening to something on the internet

technology scientific knowledge and advances

translucent not transparent but allows light through

velodromes an arena with special tracks for cycling

video cassettes tapes which were used to record moving pictures

Index

About the author

How did you get into writing?

I've always written things. My first "published" non-fiction (about my teacher!) was printed in my school yearbook when I was aged 6. It wasn't very good! But I didn't realise I could write as a job until I had children of my own!

Mio Debnam

What do you hope readers will get out of the book?

I want readers to say, "Wow! That's interesting, I didn't know that!" then want to learn even more about the subject!

Is there anything in this book that relates to your own experiences?

I've always loved discovering how things were invented. I'd love to invent something that changes people's lives!

What is it like for you to write?

When I get a good idea, I get so excited I can't wait to do research and write. The editing takes a long time, though, as I rewrite bits over and over to make them better. That's not so exciting but it's satisfying when I finish.

What is a book you remember loving reading when you were young?

I loved animal books like, *The Trumpet of the Swan* and *Charlotte's Web*, both by EB White, and *Mrs Frisby and the Rats of NIMH* by Robert O'Brien. I also adored David Attenborough's *Life on Earth*.

Why this did you decide to write this book?

Because I was really interested in how things, especially cameras and phones, were invented and developed over the years … and I wanted to share my fascination!

What's your favourite invention from the book? Why?

Cameras — because I'm a keen photographer. I got my first camera aged 13, and loved taking photos and developing them too!

Which of the inventors did you most enjoy writing about?

I was most surprised to learn about early contact lenses as I thought they were a modern invention. I couldn't believe the inventor believed in his invention so much that he was willing to use hot wax to stick them to his own eyeballs!

Book chat

What did you know about these objects before reading the book?

Why do you think the book is called *Game Changers*?

If you had to give the book a new title, what would you choose?

What have you learnt from reading this book?

If you could change one thing about this book, what would it be?

Which part of the book did you like best, and why?

What experiences have you had of the inventions in this book?

Which invention do you like best? Why?

Had you heard of any of the inventors in this book before reading it?

Would you like to try out any of the inventions in this book?

If you could ask the author one question, what would you ask?

If you could talk to one of the inventors in the book, what would you want to talk about?

What was the most interesting or surprising thing you learned from reading this book?

Would you recommend this book to a friend? Why or why not?

What are the biggest changes from the early inventions to the new objects?

Can you see any similarities in how different objects change over time?

Book challenge:

Find an object in your home and see what you can find out about its history.

Collins

BIG CAT

Author: Mio Debnam
Publisher: Lizzie Catford
Product manager and commissioning editor: Caroline Green
Series editor: Charlotte Raby
Development editor: Catherine Baker
Project manager: Emily Hooton
Content editor: Daniela Mora Chavarría
Copyeditor: Sally Byford
Proofreader: Gaynor Spry
Picture researcher: Sophie Hartley
Cover designer: Sarah Finan
Typesetter: 2Hoots Publishing Services Ltd
Production controller: Katharine Willard

Published by Collins
An imprint of HarperCollins*Publishers*
The News Building
1 London Bridge Street
London SE1 9GF
UK

Macken House
39/40 Mayor Street Upper
Dublin 1
D01 C9W8
Ireland

Download the teaching notes and word cards to accompany this book at:
http://littlewandle.org.uk/signupfluency/

Get the latest Collins Big Cat news at
collins.co.uk/collinsbigcat

MIX
Paper | Supporting responsible forestry

FSC
www.fsc.org
FSC™ C007454

This book is produced from independently certified FSC™ paper to ensure responsible forest management.

For more information visit:
www.harpercollins.co.uk/green

Collins would like to thank the teachers and children at the following schools who took part in the trialling of Big Cat for Little Wandle Fluency: Burley And Woodhead Church of England Primary School; Chesterton Primary School; Lady Margaret Primary School; Little Sutton Primary School; Parsloes Primary School.

Printed and bound in the UK using 100% Renewable Electricity at Martins the Printers Ltd

Acknowledgements
The publishers gratefully acknowledge the permission granted to reproduce the copyright material in this book. Every effort has been made to trace copyright holders and to obtain their permission for the use of copyright material. The publishers will gladly receive any information enabling them to rectify any error or omission at the first opportunity.

Front cover: bl & p42 Aleksey Boldin/Alamy; tl, title page & p79tc hoch2wo/Alamy; tr Shotshop GmbH/Alamy; bc trekandshoot/Alamy; br incamerastock/Alamy; tc Chris Willson/Alamy; back cover: tl & p79t Gallo Gusztav/Alamy; tc Science & Society Picture Library/Getty Images; tr Felix Choo/Alamy; bl & p21 SSPL/Science Museum; bc Science History Images/Alamy; br Some Wonderful Old Things/Alamy; pi & p19 pryzmat/Shutterstock, p2tl The Print Collector/Alamy, p2tr & p61 RBM Vintage Images/Alamy, p2b Simon Collins/Shutterstock, p3t & p66 ClassicStock/Alamy, p3b & p40t IanDagnall Computing/Alamy, p5 Victoria Gardner/Alamy, p6 Heritage Images/Contributor/Getty Images, p7 Artokoloro/Alamy, p8 Fox Photos/Stringer/Alamy, p9t ClassicStock/Alamy, p9b INTERFOTO/Alamy, p10 Granger/Shutterstock, p11 thislife pictures/Alamy, p18 Andrew Roland/Alamy, p22 Chronicle/Alamy, p23r Vintage Images/Alamy, p25 VI-Images/Contributor/Getty Images, p27 ZUMA Press Inc/Alamy, p28 Jon Sparks/Alamy, p30b Courtesy University of South Australia, p31t Douglas Carr/Alamy, p31b FPG/Staff/Getty Images, p32 Heritage Image Partnership Ltd /Alamy, p34 DEA/G. SIOEN/Contributor/Getty Images, p39t planetobserver/Science Photo Library, p39b Oleksiy Maksymenko Photography/Alamy, p42 Aleksey Boldin/Alamy, p44 Chris Craggs/Alamy, p45l Ecombetz/Wikimedia, p47 public domain sourced/access rights from UtCon Collection/Alamy, p49 Science Photo Library, p51 clu/Getty Images, p52 The J. Paul Getty Museum, Los Angeles, p53 f8 archive/Alamy, p56 Bettmann/Getty Images, p57 Pictorial Press Ltd/Alamy, p58 Pictorial Press Ltd/Alamy, p59l Science History Images/Alamy, p59r Science & Society Picture Library/Getty Images, p60 Sueddeutsche Zeitung Photo/Alamy, p62 Science & Society Picture Library/Getty Images, p65 Shawshots/Alamy, p67 Robert Kneschke/Alamy, p68 Artem Furman/Alamy, p69 Science History Images/Alamy, p71l Frank Nowikowski/Alamy, p71r Anyka/Alamy, p72 North Wind Picture Archives/Alamy, p73 Glasshouse Images/Alamy, p74 ARCHIVIO GBB/Alamy, p75 incamerastock/Alamy, p76 American Photo Archive/Alamy, p77l ClassicStock/Alamy, p77r ClassicStock/Alamy, p78 Classic Picture Library/Alamy, p79b Judith Collins/Alamy, p81c ArieStudio/Alamy, p82t Scott Camazine/Alamy, p82b Nigel Cattlin/Alamy, all other photos Shutterstock.